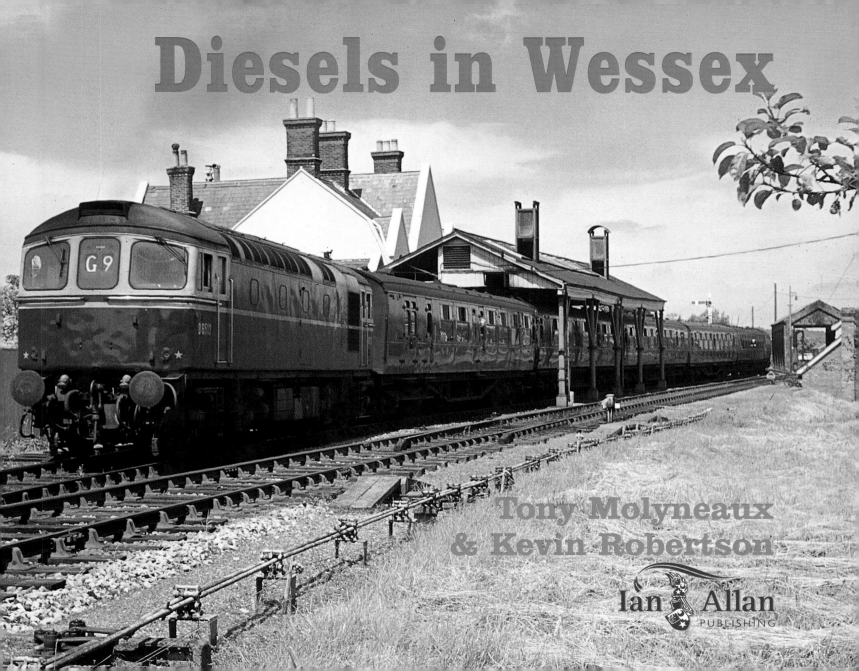

Diesels in Wessex

Tony Molyneaux
& Kevin Robertson

Ian Allan
PUBLISHING

Introduction

The area of Wessex is ill defined in today's geography books and atlases. Historically believed to refer to that portion of England encompassing the modern counties of Hampshire, Dorset, Wiltshire, Berkshire, parts of Oxfordshire, Gloucestershire, Somerset and Devon, its true boundaries are now lost in the interpretation generations of historians have given to the land formerly ruled by the various kings who have held the title 'Ruler of Wessex'.

In more recent times the railway history of the Wessex area was dominated by two renowned companies, the Great Western and the Southern, each an amalgamation of numerous smaller organisations, meaning that duplication of routes occurred. Locations such as Plymouth, Exeter, Weymouth, Salisbury and Basingstoke had for decades offered a choice to passengers as regards their preferred means of travel to London, although it would take a very loyal (or foolhardy?) traveller to venture from Salisbury to London via the Great Western compared with the direct route available from the Southern.

The duplication of services coincided basically with the life of the steam engines that hauled them. The advent of the 1955 Modernisation Plan was destined to change not only the motive power but also to rationalise the network into something more in keeping with what was then considered necessary.

Enter upon the scene the replacement motive power from 1955 onwards. As far as the Western Region was concerned this involved the early 'Warship' diesels, followed by a second, more successful series of 'Warships' and then the uniquely designed 'Hymek' and 'Western' classes. Thus steam was displaced very early on from the main routes from Paddington through Wessex, and accordingly by the early 1960s it was these classes of locomotive that formed the mainstay of express motive power on the Region.

The main line west from Waterloo fared slightly differently. Here more modern steam engines were available: rebuilt Bulleid Pacifics — in all but name brand-new engines — were in charge of services to the Dorset coast and into Wiltshire, and, although the lifetime of steam was certainly limited, until 1963 it was not even certain whether replacement would be in the form of diesel or electric traction. *Modern Railways* for the period commented that steam would be likely to last longer if the latter form of motive power were chosen, as it would take longer to provide the necessary infrastructure. Such a prophecy was correct, for, with electrification eventually chosen to Bournemouth, it was not until the summer of 1967 that steam was finally banished from Wessex, although it had already become a memory to anyone living west of Weymouth. Diesel traction was, however, selected for the ex-LSWR line from Salisbury (by now in the hands of the Western Region), in the form of

---

Front cover: Templecombe, 1 October 1966. 'Warship' No D827 *Kelly* passes over the Somerset & Dorset line in charge of the 11.00 Waterloo–Exeter. The remaining sections of the S&D were at this time in their death-throes; no longer would the 'Pines Express' be seen thundering through the arches beneath the Southern main line.

Previous page: Lymington Town on 2 July 1966, and No D6512 is seen leaving with the 12.00 from Waterloo, having called at Southampton Central and Brockenhurst only — next stop Lymington Pier in two minutes! The coaches appear to be pure Bulleid, which type remained in service on these workings until July 1967.

First published 2004

ISBN 0 7110 3010 3

Published by Ian Allan Publishing

an imprint of Ian Allan Publishing Ltd, Hersham, Surrey KT12 4RG.
Printed by Ian Allan Printing Ltd, Hersham, Surrey KT12 4RG.

Code: 0406/B1

'Warships', 'D65xx' (Class 33) and, much later, Class 50s, all of which are illustrated within these pages.

At any period in time a cursory glance at the railway scene will also perhaps give the first impression that it is a bland landscape with little in the way of variety. Such was the accusation at the time — 'Oh no, not another Warship/Class 33'; indeed, such comments are heard today as well, albeit, of course, with differing motive power being criticised. But, regardless of the period, to possess such a viewpoint is to give only a superficial glance at the actual scene — unusual workings, trial runs, through trains, all contribute to the tremendous variety that still exists. It was exactly these types of workings from the late 1950s and for about the next 30 years that Tony Molyneaux set out to record — as well, of course, as the everyday travel scene.

In compiling a pictorial record of almost any subject, there is a temptation to include solely the unusual rather than what is perceived as the mundane, yet the two should have equal billing; without one the other would not exist. Accordingly the balance of photographs selected has been towards capturing the railway in its usual workaday scene as well as the Saturday-only duties, one-offs and special workings. On such trains a variety of motive power would be seen; one can only imagine the harassed shed foreman or train manager desperately searching for a crew familiar with a particular type of motive power at a time when modern traction required a more technical approach to the driver's art.

Another theme that emerges when viewing the photographs selected occurs when those of trains actually standing or arriving at the various rural locations are identified; the views of Kingham and Chandler's Ford stand out in this respect. It has oft been quoted that, as a result of the Beeching axe of the 1960s, services were curtailed without cause and lines and intermediate stations on through routes closed. But look carefully at the illustrations and notice what are conspicuous by their absence — passengers. The diesel locomotive or diesel train may have replaced steam, but what was the point in running any train if there were no passengers to travel in it?

Contemporary with this period of change on the railway were a number of photographers determined to record what were almost daily variations. Names such as Les Elsey, Peter Gray and Bill Jackson are, of course, synonymous with the quality views we now see of the period, but there were others too. One of these is Tony Molyneaux, a friend of those mentioned above but whose work has, until now, enjoyed only very limited coverage in the railway press. Tony lived in Chandler's Ford for many years and set for himself the same high standards we have come to expect from those premier photographers of the period. Poor composition and bad exposure were just not acceptable — indeed, in searching out the views for this compilation, on more than one occasion I have been taken to task with the words 'You can't use *that* one!'

Unlike other men elsewhere, Tony was quick to appreciate that not only was it important that the steam be recorded on film but also the then modern scene. Indeed, this has been the continuing theme throughout his photographic career, which also saw him taking thousands of black-and-white photographs.

Given that he was for many years a leading member of the local group of the RCTS in Eastleigh and a member of the national RCTS photographic portfolio, it is perhaps surprising that few of Tony's colour or black-and-white views have been seen before, and it was thus with great pleasure that I accepted the invitation to collaborate on this compilation of his work.

I first made Tony's acquaintance some 20 years ago, at a time when I was heavily involved in the search for photographs in connection with another project. What I discovered was not the availability of a single view but instead an almost totally unpublished archive amassed by a quiet, unassuming man who had roamed widely over the South of England, recording not only the railway scenes but also aircraft and shipping.

For this book I have had free access to the complete slide collection, and it was all too easy to become side-tracked over differing themes. We eventually settled on the basic 'green diesel' era as a starting point (although whatever was chosen would mean many hundreds more superb views of the steam era must, for the present, go unseen). We thus have clean diesels, diesels on trial, diesels on services over routes now long forgotten as well as the early diesel scene on what was still essentially a steam-age railway.

The results, then, are solely the work of Tony Molyneaux. It has been my privilege to undertake the compilation and captioning, Tony's records allowing detail to be added to the shots. For one who witnessed the period (but was still at the 'box-brownie' stage, whereby photographic results came more by luck than judgement) this has also been something of an exercise in nostalgia; I have to admit that scenes I can actually recall mean more than those I could only imagine.

The 'green diesel' era is certainly one now viewed with affection by many — as, indeed, is the blue/grey period, devotees of which are not forgotten either, for the last few pages have been carefully selected to afford a glimpse of this scene too. Looking back, the heyday of the 'Warships', 'D65xx' and various first-generation diesel units is 20-30 years in the past, and, whilst most of those seen in these pages have long since been consigned to the scrap-heap, this book should provide an enduring record.

Kevin Robertson
Bishops Waltham
January 2004

Above: Our look at the diesel scene in Wessex commences with this delightful portrait of BRCW Type 3 'Crompton' No D6505 passing Stoneham sidings, south of Eastleigh, on a summer's evening in June 1962. The train consists of empty tanks destined for Fawley and may well have come south off the DN&S line from Didcot. Dating from World War 2, Stoneham sidings had been installed to relieve congestion at the Eastleigh bottleneck and were used for both freight and locomotive stabling. By the 1950s the sidings had fallen into disuse, but

the rusty rails remained *in situ* until parts of the site were used for a mobile welding plant in connection with the electrification of the Bournemouth line in 1967.

Right: Passenger work this time, 'Crompton' No D6554 having just entered the four-track section south of Shawford with a Waterloo–Lymington working on 1 June 1963. Judging by the open windows on the first Maunsell coach, this was obviously a hot summer's day.

Above: No D6579 on a Class 6 freight working from Feltham to Eastleigh. This was a part-fitted train, with a fitted head (possibly empty banana vans) coupled immediately next to the engine. The view was recorded at Otterbourne, north of Eastleigh, on 19 October 1963.

Above right: The Fawley oil trains had been steam-hauled between Fawley and Eastleigh until the early 1960s, when certain workings succumbed to 'Crompton' haulage. With its obligatory pair of barrier wagons, No D6546 is depicted passing under Campbell Road bridge and alongside the Eastleigh Works office block on 5 April 1963.

Right: Lymington Town station, with a rather grimy No D6520 at the head of what is no doubt a through working to Waterloo. For many years the province of elderly Drummond 4-4-0s, through workings onto the branch had for a short time been the responsibility of the 'Schools' class before being taken over by BR Standard steam types. With an ever-increasing fleet of diesels available, rostering of the new type of traction took place, and scenes such as this, recorded on 2 July 1966, were commonplace in the mid-1960s. The headcode displayed is somewhat puzzling, '2A' referring to perishables between Waterloo and Poole!

7

Left: On 17 July 1965 No D6526 heads east past Millbrook signalbox, having just left Southampton Western Docks. Today this location is the site of Millbrook Freightliner terminal (to the right) and the Maritime Freightliner depot (on the left).

Below left: Proving that green diesels could also be grimy, No D6520 is caught by the evening sun approaching Worting Junction with a mixed freight from Feltham to Eastleigh on 5 June 1964. Introduced from 1960, the 98 members of this class — referred to initially as 'D65s' and later as 'Cromptons' — were in the main seen on freight workings, their greater availability consigning to history a number of pre-Grouping steam classes.

Right: 'Crompton' No D6556 assists Bulleid 'Battle of Britain' Pacific No 34064 *Fighter Command* with the 09.30 Waterloo–Bournemouth, recorded just south of Eastleigh on 24 April 1966. Double-heading of any passenger working on the Southern was rare and generally occurred only when the train engine was an ailing locomotive in need of assistance. This was a little unusual for No 34064, however; unique among its class in being fitted with a Giesl oblong ejector in place of the standard Bulleid blastpipe, it had long been regarded by many as the best of all the SR's Pacifics. However, at the time of this photograph the locomotive was less than a month from withdrawal and thus was probably in far from the best of condition.

Right: Another diesel-and-steam combination, recorded on the same day and at the same location, this time 'Crompton' No D6555 piloting 'West Country' No 34017 *Ilfracombe* on the down 'Bournemouth Belle'. This time, however, the train engine appears to have steam to spare, so the double-heading may simply have been a means of avoiding line occupancy by a light-engine working.

A final combination of steam and diesel, also (somewhat unusually for the Southern Region at this time) featuring the new blue-and-grey-liveried coaches. That in itself dates the picture as having been taken very late in the life of steam, and Tony's records confirm that the photograph was taken on 11 June 1967 — less than a month before SR steam finished. 'Crompton' No D6501 and 'West Country' No 34093 (by then nameless but formerly *Saunton*) are seen near Southampton Airport with the 10.30 service from Waterloo to Bournemouth via Alton.

The first change of livery for the 'Cromptons' occurred as early as 1962, when No D6530 appeared at Eastleigh sporting a yellow panel at each end. However, it was some time before others of the class were so treated, as was the case with sister engine No D6533 behind. Alongside, No D6583 is keeping its front-end colour scheme to itself! This scene was recorded at the diesel depot on 14 October 1962.

11

Above: Micheldever, 4.40pm on Sunday 9 July 1967 — the last day loco-hauled Bulleid coaches would be seen on regular passenger duties on the Southern. No D6510 is photographed at the head of what is at least a 10-coach train — including two BR Mk 1 vehicles — and with the new '91' headcode which described the fast services between Bournemouth and Waterloo in either direction.

Right: Three 'Cromptons' again in this the last view of the type in green, this time with all three clearly indicating differing painting styles. Nos D6518, with full yellow ends, and D6501 head south past Eastleigh depot on 29 April 1967 as an unidentified member of the class with a yellow panel awaits the all-clear to leave the shed roads. The train is a mixed freight, possibly destined for Northam yard, of a type which would disappear completely from the scene within a couple of years.

Above: The first regular diesel workings in the Hampshire part of Wessex commenced in 1958 with the introduction of two- (later three-) car diesel-electric units for local and branch-line use. The new trains meant the end for many of the elderly push-pull branch-line engines, 'M7' duties from Eastleigh now being severely restricted. Perhaps surprisingly, however, the diesel services were initially confined to central Hampshire, and Bournemouth shed continued to provide steam for its branch-line services almost to the very end. With its non-powered driving trailer leading, unit No 1116 enters Fareham with an Eastleigh–Portsmouth service on 28 October 1962.

Above right: Portsmouth was also served by diesel trains from Southampton, Reading, Salisbury and Andover, although the latter ceased with the closure of the 'Sprat & Winkle' line in 1964. No 1132, a three-coach unit, is seen coming off the Andover line and joining the

Salisbury–Romsey route at Kimbridge Junction on 18 April 1964. Trains operating from Andover this way would travel to Portsmouth via Romsey, Chandler's Ford and Eastleigh; Chandler's Ford would later close as a station, although the line itself remained open. Nearly 40 years later, in 2003, a new station would be opened at Chandler's Ford, albeit no longer served by 'Hampshire' units or trains running via Clatford, Fullerton, Stockbridge, Horsebridge and Mottisfont.

Right: Soon after entering traffic, unit 1115, later strengthened with the addition of a centre coach, enters what was then Platform 2 at Eastleigh. At the time it was a requirement for the units to display an old-style oil lamp on the rear, even though the indicator blinds could well have been used for a more effective red display. The train is probably destined for Winchester or Alton, diesel traction having taken over services to/from both very early on.

Above: Eastleigh station this time and another three-car set displaying the '76' headcode indicative of an Alton–Southampton working. The train is at Platform 3, the remainder of the station being temporarily bereft of traffic. The unit is believed to be No 1103, a regular performer. All the units were based at Eastleigh diesel depot for servicing and maintenance.

Above right: Typical of the units working the Alton line, No 1110 arrives at Ropley *en route* to Southampton. For many years it had been the practice to limit trains on this line to two-coach sets, primarily because of the severe gradients, which could be taxing for the limited power available. However, the diesel sets generated additional traffic, and later years saw three-coach trains, albeit with engines that had been uprated slightly. Today Ropley is the location of the Mid Hants

Railway's locomotive shed and workshops and has considerably more track and infrastructure than are apparent in this 3 November 1963 view.

Right: On 3 November 1963 two-car DEMU No. 1115 leaves Ropley heading north for Medstead and Alton in what was then deepest rural Hampshire. The guard has yet to close his inward-opening door, contemporary practice being to stand in the open doorway to observe a safe departure — Health & Safety please note! The orange 'V' on the front was a relatively recent addition and was intended to serve two purposes — principally to identify to station staff the end of the set where the guard's/luggage compartment was located but also as an early form of warning to permanent-way gangs of the train's approach.

Below: Unit 1103 resplendent in smart green livery; eagle-eyed viewers will note the BR emblem appears only on the first (motor) vehicle. The set is running on the up through line between Eastleigh and Allbrook Junction, with the East Yard's reception sidings full — as, indeed, they always seemed to be in the early 1960s. To the right are the up relief and up goods loop lines, the latter used mainly as a layby for the Fawley oil trains when both up routes were busy.

Right: On the easily graded Eastleigh–Fareham section No 1113 takes the single-line tunnel route towards Fareham, with Knowle Halt just visible in the background. To the left are the parallel tracks of the Fareham Tunnel-avoiding lines, which would be abandoned following construction of the M27 motorway between Portsmouth and Southampton.

Left: Reopened in May 2003, Chandler's Ford station is today vastly different from the original, depicted here in 1963. This is a down (Eastleigh-direction) working, consisting of two three-car units, with No 1109 leading. Multiple working of these units was never a common feature.

Below: No 1102 near Flexford, east of Romsey, *c*1962, apparently shortly after repaint. Aside from the smart unit the whole railway scene was still one of neatness at the time; the latter-day overgrown banks and uncut vegetation would have caused contemporary gangers and civil engineers to shudder.

Above: By the time the Oxted-line units were being built in 1962, the front end design of the DEMU sets had been altered slightly to give a more curved appearance compared with the somewhat angular front ends of the 'Hampshire' sets. There were also minor changes in the location of passenger facilities, including the toilet, although none of these was ever really appreciated by the Hampshire passengers, as, aside from trial and running-in turns, the sets rarely worked in the Eastleigh area. Unit No 1304 is seen on trial north of Eastleigh on 23 May 1962.

Right: Our final view of the DEMU type shows two Oxted-line units — Nos 1315 and 1317 — at Southampton Central in August 1966; the working is unknown. The conductor rail for the 1967 electrification is already in place, whilst the clock tower is in the process of being demolished to make way for a modern concrete office block.

23

Above: With the abolition of steam on the Southern Region replacements for the various steam types that had loyally shunted the docks for many years were required, and these came in the form of a number of 0-6-0 diesels built by Ruston & Hornsby. Their role was short-lived, however, rapid global containerisation meaning the need for shunting wagons was almost past. No D2987 is seen in the Eastern Docks in late February 1965.

Above right: Apparently brand-new, No D2998 is seen at work in Southampton Docks c1962. The red coupling-rods set off the colour

scheme to advantage, although they seldom remained for long in this pristine condition. This particular engine seemed to spend long periods shunting Tipton Yard (Eastleigh) around this time and may well have been used for crew-training purposes.

Right: Old and new together: 'USA' tank No 30069 and Ruston & Hornsby diesel shunter No D2993 at Southampton Docks in May 1963. No prizes for guessing which was the more popular with crews! Notice the shunter's pole slung across the buffers of the 'Ruston'.

25

Below: Newly delivered English Electric 0-6-0 diesel-electric shunter No D3719 stands outside Eastleigh steam shed in 1959. In the background (left) is a very clean unrebuilt 'Battle of Britain' Bulleid Pacific, No 34079 *141 Squadron*, while just discernible on the right are a rebuilt Bulleid and an 'M7' 0-4-4T, with what appears to be a Brighton tank completing the picture.

Right: Whilst, in their earliest days, the diesel-electric shunters were sometimes to be seen on local trip and engineer's workings, such duties became less common due to higher train speeds and the inability of the shunting engines to travel at more than about 12mph. Nevertheless No D3019 is shown here a few miles from Eastleigh, at Halterworth (near Romsey) with a permanent-way special in June 1963.

For a time in the late 1950s some of the BR-built Type 2 diesel-electric locomotives in the 'D51xx' series could be seen at work in the Kent area of the Southern Region, but all later migrated north of the Thames, a number working on the Eastern Region from King's Cross. They had always been a rare sight in the Wessex area, although No D5146 was captured approaching Winchester with an excursion from Berkhamstead on 16 June 1962.

To supplement the diminishing fleet of available steam locomotives (which were also becoming less and less reliable due to shortage of spares and limitations on repairs) the Southern Region was compelled to borrow a number of Brush Type 4 diesels for use both locally and also on the through inter-Regional workings. No D1805 was photographed just north of St Denys with a Midlands/North of England working — possibly the re-routed 'Pines Express' — on 17 July 1965.

No D1740 in charge of an Eastleigh-bound freight near Otterbourne, recorded at 18.40 on 2 May 1965. Although the Brush Type 4s were intended as a mixed-traffic locomotives, they were seldom seen on non-passenger workings on the SR at this time.

The sight of a diesel locomotive hauling the very last 'Bournemouth Belle' on Sunday 9 July 1967 — the very last day of steam working on the region — was the cause of much regret for many enthusiasts, most having hoped that the authorities would roster steam for this final sad occasion. It was not to be, however, and Brush Type 4 No D1924 was assigned to the final up working, seen near Micheldever. The Full Brake (leading) was provided as there were then few Pullman Brake Seconds available (as had been the case for some time). Usually, however, a Full Brake in chocolate-and-cream was included which allowed for a more pleasing match to the accompanying coaching stock.

Left: Away from the Southern now and towards the Western Region's part of Wessex. Where better to start than at Swindon, where on 1 April 1962, North British Type 2 diesel-hydraulic No D6340 is posed alongside No 4920 *Dumbleton Hall*, both seemingly fresh from overhaul and in marked contrast to the row of work-stained engines behind.

Below: Three BR-built 0-6-0 shunters — Nos D2194, D2146, and D2198 — of a 1957 design featuring a 204hp Gardner engine driving through mechanical transmission. They were intended for light shunting duties, but the rapid closure of goods yards and the spread of block working soon rendered them redundant from the modern railway scene, and most were destined to last little longer than the steam engines they were intended to replace. The trio are seen at Swindon on 28 May 1961.

Left: The GWR had been the largest user of diesel units before BR came upon the scene, and indeed some of the originals dating from the mid-1930s were still in service almost 30 years later. Here a three-coach set is seen in the down bay at Reading General in August 1959. The middle coach is a standard Collett with through wiring to the power cars at each end; leading the formation is vehicle W38.

Above: The end of the road for ex-GWR diesel unit W21W, awaiting the cutter's torch at Swindon in March 1963. Clearly then not all the WR units were repainted in the BR standard green used for multiple-units, and this particular car had been stored out of service for some time.

Moving northwest now to another part of Wessex but still on the Western Region. On 28 April 1963 Tony Molyneaux visited Wantage Road, where he recorded 'Warship' diesel-hydraulic No D839 *Relentless* passing the signalbox with the late-running 1A66 (10.35amSO Taunton–Paddington) service, part of which is formed of maroon-liveried Hawksworth stock.

'Warship' No D826 *Jupiter* heads west past Wantage Road, on the WR main line between Didcot and Swindon, on 28 April 1963. The headcode poses something of a problem, being conspicuous by its absence from the contemporary working timetable, although, judging from the rake of smart Mk 1 coaches, this is a prestige working, probably to the West Country.

Above left: By 1960 the 'Torbay Express' had already been given over to diesel haulage, such was the speed of progress in the WR modernisation scheme. 'Warship' No D820 *Grenville* was in charge near Aller Junction (Newton Abbot) on 14 July 1960, the locomotive being in its original livery of all-over green with white waistband. The continued use of an old-style steam headboard will be noted, as will the rake of smart chocolate-and-cream Mk 1 coaches.

Left: West of Newton Abbot again on the same day, and No D817 *Foxhound* has charge of the 11.38 Newton Abbot–Plymouth service with a mixed maroon and chocolate-and-cream rake. Strict limitations

on the loadings of the diesel-hauled services west from Newton Abbot meant that instances of double-heading over the South Devon banks were curtailed, bringing considerable savings both in locomotive running and in finding return paths.

Above: Transfer of the former SR line west of Salisbury to WR control in 1964 also meant the replacement of steam on the Waterloo–Exeter services by 'Warship' diesel-hydraulics, which themselves had now been ousted from front-line WR duties by the newer 'Westerns'. No D831 *Monarch* is seen at Tisbury, still with a rake of SR Bulleid coaches in tow.

Left: Another view of No D831 *Monarch*, this time at Semley on 29 August 1964. The green rake has been supplemented by a single WR-liveried vehicle, then an unusual sight on the SR.

Below: Understandably the busy junction at Reading was a Mecca for spotters and photographers alike. This scene was recorded on 9 August 1962, with No D807 *Caradoc* in charge of a Weston-super-Mare–Paddington service and displaying 'A' class headcode discs as the first 12 'Warships' were built with by-then disused steam-style 3-character stencil frames instead of the later four-digit display. The motley rake of coaching stock is also worthy of study, as are the semaphore signals, which would disappear from Reading within a few years.

Above left: An unusual working for No D802 *Formidable* northbound on the approach to Southampton Airport on 26 April 1967. The train is a part-fitted freight, the box vans preceding a long rake of coal empties possibly destined for Basingstoke. At this time freight workings in Hampshire were usually in the hands of 'Cromptons' or even ageing steam types, so the 'Warship' may well have been used to avoid a light-engine return from an unbalanced working.

Left: The same locomotive photographed the previous year on a much lighter working. No D802 *Formidable* is seen at Worting Junction, near Basingstoke, with an Exeter–Waterloo service on 14 August 1966. The

first three members of the class were slightly less powerful (2,000hp), but even so a load of just four coaches would have made timing such a train a comparatively simple task, paths permitting!

Above: Our final view of a 'Warship' in maroon livery depicts No D817 *Foxhound*, seemingly attracting the attention of a number of enthusiasts at the west end of Salisbury station in late December 1968. By now many of the class had received full yellow ends, this being an interim stage prior to the application of corporate Rail blue to match the livery already carried here by the coaching stock. Note in the background the former GWR signalbox.

New motive power at Swindon steam shed in 1963. 'Hymek' diesel-hydraulics Nos D7074, D7053 and a rather grimy D7050 stand outside the shed whilst another, unidentified member of the class lurks within on 30 March, when none was more than a few months old.

Among the principal duties assigned to the 'Hymeks' were the services between Worcester and Paddington. An unidentified member of the class is seen at speed near Charlbury with a nine-coach train for Paddington on 29 July 1963.

Below: A heavy load for No D7010 as it cautiously enters the up main platform at Reading on 9 August 1962 with train 1A26, the 7.30am Swansea–Paddington working.

Right: Moreton-in-Marsh in the summer of 1963, with another member of the class — regrettably unidentified — about to pass through the station with a train for Worcester. At this time this section of the former 'Old Worse and Worse' (Oxford–Worcester–Wolverhampton) route was still double-track throughout, although much of it would later be singled. Forty years on, both the locomotive type and coaching stock are but a distant memory on this line, but the signalbox and mechanical signalling survive at what remains a crossing-place.

Left: Historically a very interesting item indeed: No D1000 *Western Enterprise*, the very first of its type, brand-new in Swindon Works on 1 April 1962. The 'desert sand' livery is perhaps best described as striking; overall, however, the type is considered by many to be the most handsome diesel design ever produced.

Above: Locomotive and stock neatly matched at Bristol Temple Meads on 4 July 1964, with No D1014 *Western Firebrand* awaiting departure for Paddington. Readers should perhaps excuse the unintentional view of the individual caught bending over on the platform …

Left: The final member of its class, No D1073 *Western Bulwark*, on a special from Wolverhampton, passes green-liveried three-car 'Hampshire' DEMU No 1102 near Winchester Junction on 16 May 1964.

Above: Light-engine working between Swindon and Didcot in April 1964. Judging by the 'Z' code, No D1010 *Western Campaigner* is probably on test after repair at Swindon. The maroon livery suited the class particularly well, although, like the green, this would later give way to the inevitable Rail blue.

Left: Micheldever in September 1961, some time before track rationalisation and the installation of modern signalling. Two Reading-based three-car DMUs are seen leaving the station on a through working between Reading and Southampton Terminus — a duty then shared between steam and the new motive power. Such workings continued until *c*1963, following which a change of rosterings meant that Eastleigh-based DEMUs took over. Each type had its supporters, the Hampshire units for their generally smoother ride against the WR type, which afforded passengers with a better view all round.

Below: Seen at almost the same location but a month earlier, on 12 August 1961, another six-coach train made up of two three-car sets heads south through Micheldever and about to leave the station loop.

Left: By the early 1960s steam had also given way to the newer form of traction on local services. On 27 July 1963 a Worcester–Oxford local arrives at Finstock Halt, east of Kingham, as part of a diagram which involved the set running from Birmingham (Tyseley) and eventually returning the same day.

Above: The classic view of Torquay, recorded on 15 July 1960. An almost brand-new three-coach set on a local from either Newton Abbot or Exeter is bound for Kingswear. The contemporary motor vehicles in the car park are also worthy of more than a passing glance.

Above: A lineside permit allowed Tony access to locations barred to many and including the embankment north of Allbrook, where another WR-based DMU is seen heading north on the up fast line on its way home from Southampton Terminus in June 1961. In the background the veritable plethora of signals is indicative of the proximity of the yards and junctions at Eastleigh, part of the East Yard being just visible beyond the down main gantry.

Right: Kingham, on the Worcester line, had for many years been a junction with the Banbury–Cheltenham route, with a series of connections and flyovers provided, the size of the station itself was also totally at odds with that of the community it was intended to serve. Regrettably the arrival of diesel units did little to arrest the drop-off in traffic then being experienced, and, although the route still survives today, the station does not. This, though, was the scene in 1963, with a green unit pausing at what is clearly a deserted platform.

The former Wilts, Somerset & Weymouth line was one of the earliest railways in Dorset, and the coastal resort was for many years a GWR (and, later, WR) destination. Latterly, however, services between Weymouth and London were redirected to/from Waterloo via the Southern connection at Dorchester, with WR trains now in the hands of diesel units. A typical example was the 1.58pm Westbury–Weymouth; having passed through Frome, Castle Cary, Yeovil and Maiden Newton, this train is seen arriving at its destination on 19 July 1960.

Seldom captured on film, the 'South Wales Pullman' passes Wantage Road *en route* for Paddington. The 'Blue Pullman' trains were a short-lived venture in prestige working and operated for a time between Paddington and Birmingham and Paddington and South Wales. Although providing a standard of service equal to the best rail facilities available anywhere, they were not always popular with the fare-paying passenger, on account of their rough ride. All were subsequently withdrawn prematurely, and the later High Speed Trains (HSTs) represented a marked improvement in terms of both speed and ride quality.

Left: Introduced from 1962, the Brush Type 4 (later BR Class 47) would turn out to be one of the most numerous and long-lived of all the early diesel classes — indeed, a number still survive 40 years later, although many have been modified considerably over the years. In original condition No D1588 stands at Bristol Temple Meads on 4 July 1964 at the head of a through working from Plymouth to Liverpool.

Above: The same type of working, but this time nearly 20 years on. An unidentified class 47 at speed on the up main line near Pangbourne in 1981 on what may well be a service from Bristol.

Above left: Moving on in years now to 1979 — we shall return to the early 1970s shortly — Class 31s Nos 31 412 and 31 132 are seen stabled between duties at Swindon alongside Class 08 No 08 839. Another long-lived type, Class 31s (originally known as Brush Type 2s) were at first confined to the Eastern and North Eastern regions but later saw service on most parts of the BR network. They were not universally popular, however, Southern men comparing them unfavourably with their beloved Class 33 'Cromptons' and describing them as 'unable to pull the skin off a rice-pudding'!

Left: Although not based on the Southern for any length of time, the class had a number of regular turns, including Bristol–Portsmouth workings via Salisbury and Southampton. Seen at St Denys on 1 June

1979, No 31 243 leaves the Portsmouth line and heads for Southampton. Interestingly these trains, which ran as fixed five-coach formations, always had a Guard's Brake marshalled as the centre vehicle, so that parcels could be dealt with safely at some of the shorter platforms *en route.*

Above: Another, unidentified, '31' at Tunnel Junction, east of Salisbury, taking the route southeast towards Romsey and Southampton. As previously, the Brake will be noted towards the centre of the train, which this time is made up of more than the usual five coaches. Train identification has become more difficult following the decision to abandon displayed headcodes, although four-digit identification is still used by signalling centres to describe trains.

Above: Seen near Salisbury Tunnel Junction with an unidentified Class 33 at their head, empty ballast hoppers return westwards to Meldon Quarry, Okehampton, in September 1978.

Right: With a train of full bitumen tanks, Class 33 No 33 017 heads north alongside the River Itchen near St Denys on 1 June 1979. The extreme curvature of the erstwhile London & Southampton main line is readily apparent; further south was the even sharper curve around Northam Junction, which is still notorious for necessitating the slowest speed on any main rail route in mainland Britain.

Left: Fresh from overhaul and repaint at Eastleigh, No 33 026 arrives at its destination of Salisbury at the head of the 14.10 service from Waterloo on 22 August 1987. The Class 33s remained on these services until ousted by the larger Class 50s, which in turn were later superseded by the present generation of newer diesel units — a far cry indeed from the time when Bulleid Pacifics had charge of such trains.

Above: A final view of a blue-liveried Class 33 and a scene which can now no longer be repeated. No D6531 and '4-TC' set No 410 are posed alongside the now demolished Ocean Terminal at Southampton's Eastern Docks, once the staging-post for the numerous boat trains which met transatlantic liners. On this occasion, 1 March 1970, the train has arrived in connection with the departure of the Spanish Line's *Begoña*, although a 'TC' would have been a poor substitute for the sumptuous carriages once provided on such workings.

Left: Busy times at Bournemouth in late summer 1982. Class 47/4 No 47 484 *Isambard Kingdom Brunel* has charge of the 09.42 Poole–Newcastle as '4-VEP' unit No 7703 waits to follow with a stopping train to Waterloo. As will be gathered from the size of the gap between the platforms, Bournemouth (formerly Bournemouth Central) once boasted a pair of through lines; these were removed following electrification, leaving the site a little bare, although in recent times a serious attempt has been made to improve its image.

Above: Aside from having charge of the various inter-Regional workings from the South Coast, the Class 47 type has also been associated with the build-up of rail-borne container traffic to/from the docks at Southampton. Indeed, there is basically now a container train in each direction for each hour of the day and night. Many of these will effect a crew change at Eastleigh, as had probably occurred with No 47 534, seen leaving the down platform (now redesignated Platform 2) on 4 September 1978.

Left: Class 47 No 1740 heads into the evening sun near Halterworth Crossing on the Chandler's Ford line at the head of engineers' stock in June 1973 and before being renumbered in the TOPS series as 47 147. The versatility of this class has been remarked upon previously, and many would later be renumbered again to reflect their respective duties — freight, parcels, InterCity etc. Although the type has generally proved popular with drivers, one persistent criticism refers to draughts within the cabs, and it was not uncommon to find several spots around the driver's seat stuffed with newspapers and old service timetables!

Above: Class 47 No 1595 near Flexford (on the outskirts of Chandler's Ford) on an excursion working in June 1973. During the 1970s and '80s such trains were a regular feature of the weekend scene on the Southern Region (as indeed they were elsewhere), management being keen to gain extra revenue from hiring out coaching stock which would otherwise have stood idle.

Left: A blue 'Western' in its final years. Withdrawal of the class as non-standard had commenced as early as 1973, and as time passed the survivors were used for duties for which they had never been intended. An example of this was on stone trains such as those from Merehead to Eastleigh, Botley or Wooton Bassett. Such trains often grossed up to 2,000 tons yet were handled with consummate ease by these mighty machines. Sadly the demands placed upon transmissions, allied to ever-reducing maintenance, took their toll, and with limited repairs authorised the sight of a 'Western' on a stone train really signified it was being worked to its end. No D1005 *Western Venturer* was just 18 months from withdrawal when photographed near Romsey while *en route* to Botley in July 1975.

Below: 'Warship' No D846 *Steadfast* on a through WR–SR parcels, probably from Reading, caught near the erstwhile Stoneham sidings south of Eastleigh in February 1969.

Left: Following their demise from front-line duty on the WR in consequence of the introduction of the HST, a number of Class 50s were drafted onto the Waterloo–Exeter services, with the result that for the first time major improvements were possible to the timetable. Unfortunately, however, the earlier track singling west of Salisbury prevented the type's full potential from being realised, although the sight of a '50' in full flight quickly attracted a loyal band of enthusiastic followers. No 50 008 *Thunderer* is seen at Salisbury with the 13.10 Waterloo–Exeter not long after the class first appeared, on 19 June 1982.

Below: The location — Great Bedwyn, on the Berks & Hants main line — is unmistakable, although the motive power is a bit unusual, to say the least! 'Deltic' No 55 016 *Gordon Highlander* was recorded on an enthusiasts' special working on 28 November 1981 — shortly before withdrawal, which came the following month.

Left: The versatility of the SR's '4-TC' trailer units is demonstrated by set No 428, being propelled by a push-pull-fitted Class 33 near Romsey on a diverted Bournemouth–Waterloo working in April 1982. Subsequent electrification of the coast route between Southampton and Portsmouth has resulted in a much greater flexibility of working during periods of engineers' occupation and the like, and, although certain diverted passenger services still use the Romsey connection, this has dwindled in recent years.

Above: A two-car DEMU, probably No 1121 or No 1122 — each being a common sight in Hampshire for many years — recorded broadside in all-over blue livery from Shawford Down in May 1967. This was the first livery change to the sets after green, although later blue-and-grey was carried.

Left: No record of the SR scene would be complete without a photograph of the electro-diesel type. No E6020 of the second batch leaves the Western Dock at Southampton on a Waterloo-bound boat train, where (for the present, at least) the limited power — just 600hp — of its diesel engine will be no handicap, due to the slow speeds necessary for the sharp curves. The coaching stock is an interesting mix of styles, the colourful combination being recorded on 4 June 1967.

Below left: Wrong-line working over the down main at Eastleigh in July 1976, seen from Bishopstoke Road overbridge. Regrettably the identity of the electro-diesel was not recorded, although its destination was no doubt the East Yard, reached via a series of crossovers just north of the station.

To complement the smaller 'EDs' a number of larger, more powerful units were converted from redundant South Eastern-section electric locomotives in the 'E50xx' series. They were intended for use primarily on boat trains, but such duties disappeared quicker than the railway could have envisaged, and the class was left with limited work through the 1970s. Noted for being particularly fast — one former Eastleigh driver recalls he had one 'way off the clock' — they were affectionately known as 'Spin Dryers', a curious reference to the noise created by the auxiliary diesel engines. Shortly after this view was recorded at Eastleigh in September 1977 most of the class were to be found dumped at the nearby diesel depot, where they were to remain for some time pending a decision as to their fate. In the end it was to the scrap heap that the call came. Whoever said the modern scene stands still?

Index of Locations Illustrated

Back cover: By 1966 new instructions had been issued abolishing the need for barrier wagons when tanker trains were hauled by diesel or electric traction, as demonstrated by 'Crompton' No D6595 wending its way cautiously west towards Southampton Central on 20 August. The engine would also appear to have recently received a repaint — almost certainly its last in green and this time adorned with a larger yellow front panel, silver roof and red buffer-beam. To the right the relative quiet of Civic Centre Road is disturbed by only a few cars. The skyline of the city would change considerably over the years with the demolition of the old power station (right) to make way for a prestigious shopping centre.